The heart of NEW ENGLAND

MALLARD PRESS
An imprint of BDD Promotional Book Company, Inc.,
666 Fifth Avenue,
New York, N.Y. 10103

Mallard Press and its accompanying duck logo are
registered trademarks of
BDD Promotional Book Company, Inc.
Registered in the U.S. Patent and Trademark Office.

CLB 3161
© 1993 Colour Library Books Ltd.,
Godalming, Surrey, England
First published in the United States of America 1993
by The Mallard Press
Printed and bound in Singapore
All rights reserved
ISBN 0 7924 5829 X

Of the two towns on Maine's Deer Isle, Stonington
(previous page) is the newer. Its harbor is filled
with lobster boats, but it was built as a lumber port.

Red leaves, white churches and covered bridges are
as much symbols of New England as hard-working
boats, and this setting in Stark (right), New
Hampshire, provides a perfect example of just how
beautiful the combination can be.

The heart of
NEW ENGLAND

Text by
WILLIAM BIGELOW

MALLARD
PRESS

President George Bush grew up in Greenwich, Connecticut, but even after declaring himself a Texan he kept his roots intact by running up to Kennebunkport, Maine, for relaxation. His former Greenwich neighbors who get up before the sun to catch the train for New York don't seem to have a lot in common with the ones in Maine who watch the sunrise from the stern of a lobster boat rather than from a windy railroad station platform, but they do. At the bottom of it, they're all New Englanders. If the sunrise turns the sky red, they know that the rest of the day will be windy and rainy. On the other hand, they also know that if the sky is gray and tinged with red, it will be a sunny day. You don't have to be a New Englander to know that, but up in the northeast corner of the United States, folks seem to know such things instinctively. The lobsterman also knows that if he sees a one-legged seagull, a storm is coming, quite possibly what he'll call a "goose-drownder." Further down the coast in Massachusetts, flocks of gulls flying west mean the same thing. In Vermont they watch the swallows. If the birds are flying low it's probably going to rain. And if the cows are chasing each other around the pasture, you can count on it.

All New Englanders aren't the same, not by a long shot. But if the Bostonians who are finding New Hampshire an easy commute to their jobs at the Hub of the Universe find their new neighbors a bit peculiar, and Nantucketers still refer to Cape Cod as "the continent," even newcomers pick up expressions they all understand. Sometimes they might find themselves cautioning free-spending local officials not to wash more than they can hang out, and when public servants don't respond to their needs quickly enough, they accuse them of being as slow as a hoptoad in wet tar. They also begin calling autumn visitors leaf-peepers and smirking about the fancy duds the summer people in their midst insist on wearing, even when their own attire is carefully coordinated by the folks at L.L. Bean up in Freeport, Maine. And even if they themselves discovered New England as leaf-peepers

and summer people, they pick up the linguistic nuances quicker than, as they say, greased lightning.

And they find much more to talk about than the weather, although the subject is pervasive. Without it, after all, where would that fall color come from? Autumn brings incredible beauty down the East Coast all the way to the Great Smoky Mountains in Tennessee, but New England seems to have a patent on the show, and New Englanders themselves are as impressed by it as any first-time visitor, even though they try to hide it by off-handedly calling it "the color." One of the reasons for the remarkable display is that, while summer is still in the southern forests, the drama is already beginning to unfold up in the Maine woods. The chemistry begins when nighttime temperatures drop below forty-five degrees and tighten the cells in leaves so that chlorophyll production is cut off. As the nights grow longer the work intensifies and, before you know it, the only green left is in the conifers, which along with the blue of the sky provide a beautiful counterpoint to the brilliant colors. But even Southern Connecticut gets a preview long before the days shorten and the birds begin flying south. It begins with the brilliant red of the sumac, a tree that qualifies as a weed the rest of the year if it is noticed at all. Before long the swamp maples get the message and they begin turning bright red, too. At about the same time, Virginia creeper clinging to the trunks of trees and tangled among evergreen branches adds flashes of red like the sparks in a bonfire. Even poison ivy that has been lurking in the sandy places gives itself away by becoming a beautiful shade of reddish-orange.

Once the stage has been set, the ash trees take on a bluish tinge and the oaks begin turning the color of rich, brown leather. Birches and sugar maples start with a dull yellow that in a few days becomes almost the color of pure gold. As they fall away, some types of oak turn crimson, others opt for maroon or a color quite close to purple. Then, much more quickly than it came, the show is over for another year.

New Hampshire's Swift River lives up to its name.

It seems as though it has been going on forever, and it is true that New England is one of the oldest areas of dry land anywhere in the world. The mountains of New Hampshire and Western Massachusetts are at least a half-billion years old, but they had no sooner pushed up out of the ocean than they began to change. Their size was increased by volcanoes, then reduced by wind and rain, but the granite that's still there resisted all the forces bent on destroying it. Then, about a million years ago, like all of North America as far west as the Great Plains, a new force came into play. It all began almost imperceptibly when the average temperature began to drop. If humans had been on the scene, they probably wouldn't have noticed, but further north it became cold enough to keep snow on the ground for most of the year, and as it piled up for hundreds of years it slowly turned to ice heavy enough to move down the mountainsides. As the ice sheet moved south it leveled mountains and carved valleys, and it pushed all the debris ahead of it to form new hills and hummocks. Every square foot of New England was covered, but the granite that has become a symbol of the New England character resisted the onslaught. It happened at least three different times over several thousand years before temperatures began to rise and the ice melted for the last time. The resulting water created the rivers and streams, lakes and ponds that make the New England landscape so charming today. Like the Biblical story of creation, the dry land was empty of vegetation and wildlife, but for all the images of fierce cold that a mile-thick ice sheet can conjure up, life was close at hand.

The temperature at the edge of the glaciers was frigid, to be sure, but warmth just beyond kept grasses and trees from dying, and as soon as the ice melted the moisture encouraged new growth. Native plants like hemlocks and pines, maples and birch were first, but the warming and the moisture also attracted such shrubs as rhododendrons and holly, and such trees as cedar and hickory that had originally evolved much further south. Their descendants have become as common in the Green Mountains and the Berkshires as in the Alleghenies.

When Europeans began arriving in the seventeenth century, the thing that impressed them most about New England was the abundance of trees. It was said that a squirrel born in Maine's North Woods could migrate all the way to the Mississippi River without ever touching the ground. But if such a feat had ever been possible, the opportunity was lost long before the Pilgrims set foot on Plymouth Rock. The Indians who preceded them were farmers, and over centuries they had burned away huge chunks of forest to create fields. There was plenty of land and they generally made new clearings each spring to get at the virgin soil. They were also hunters and flushed deer and small game from the woods by setting fire to the underbrush. The result was that by the time the white men came there were great gaps in the forest. But still, compared to the landscape of old England the new land was a woodland the like of which none of them had ever dreamed existed.

The Indians had been working for generations to clear the land, but without iron axes it probably would have taken them centuries to accomplish what the Englishmen managed in just a few years. Within a hundred years all but about a quarter of Massachusetts, Connecticut and Rhode Island was open land, mostly pastureland and small farms. In Maine, where the pine trees were ideal for making tall masts for the King's navy, the forests were declared off-limits to the locals, with the result that a relatively tiny percentage of the trees were cut. In the last century, as nature has reclaimed abandoned farms, the Maine forests are about as thick and extensive as they were three hundred years ago, and the trend has spread through almost all of New England. Cities and their suburbs, as well as villages, towns and factories, have edged out the woodlands in many corners of the region, but right now more than three quarters of New England is forested, not far from the same percentage back when it was the land of the Pilgrim's pride.

Maine's historic Port Clyde combines work and pleasure.

One of the fascinating things about tramping through the Berkshire Hills is imagining that those same paths were familiar to the last of the Mohicans, and a hiker in the mountains of Vermont can visualize Ethan Allen and his Green Mountain Boys on their way to cut off the British on Lake Champlain. It is fun to feel that it is possible, surrounded by the same trees he knew, to recreate the experiences of Henry David Thoreau, and to visit a colonial village and think of the people who watched the leaves change color so many autumns ago. Such thoughts come easily in New England, but the trees, like the people, aren't the same ones our great-grandfathers saw. The New England woodland has been cut over several times, but the good news is that it has come back over and over again, and it is getting better all the time.

But it comes back in a slightly altered form. The virgin forests included the stately elms that made main streets and village greens so beautiful a century ago, but disease has virtually wiped them out. They were also filled with chestnut trees that a blight has long-since made extinct. And the great oaks and other hardwoods often take more than a human generation to grow to maturity. The process of a forest naturally recreating itself begins with birches and pines that thrive in open sunny fields and produce heavy crops of seeds that birds spread to other open spaces. Before long they become so thick that their shade retards the growth of their seedlings, but other trees like red maples that thrive in light shade find it a perfect environment. They, in turn, cut off more sun, and the oaks and sugar maples, beech and ash, and especially hemlock, all of which need shelter to become established, start to take over. At about the same time the older birches and pines die out and a new, young forest replaces another open field.

About all that remains as a reminder that a field was once there is the stone walls. They are everywhere in New England, even deep in the woods far from any other signs of civilization. Today's New Englander treasures them, and many a gentleman farmer has hired stonecutters to build proper walls and bring solidity to the landscape. But the originals weren't built for any aesthetic reason and, indeed, many had no more practical a purpose than to provide a convenient way to get rid of the stones. Among the legacies of the great glaciers, New England's soil is filled with boulders and rocks and deep pockets of gravel, and when the early farmers cleared their fields they also had to dig out the stones in the path of their plows. It was hard work, and no one was inclined to move them any further than they had to, so they piled them at the edge of the field, usually in the form of low walls which helped keep the sheep in the meadow and the cow away from the corn, but gave deer an easy challenge and provided good cover for small animals, which probably enjoyed living so close to a handy food supply. Most of the original farms were on hillsides or at the tops of hills, because the early settlers believed that disease lurked in foggy lowlands. But the best soil was in the valleys and in the places they chose it was so thin that most were forced to abandon their enterprise after a generation or so. Most pulled up stakes and went west, and by the middle of the nineteenth century all that was left of most of the original New England farms was mile after mile of stone walls. By the 1990s only about .03 percent of New Englanders the census bureau identifies as "rural" live on working farms.

The majority of New Englanders live within smelling distance of salt water, and most of their traditions are centered on the sea. In the beginning, of course, everybody lived on the coast. The first settlers arrived by ship, and the forests beyond the coastal plain were filled with who knows what kind of wild beasts and savages. Besides, there was a living to be made from the fish in the offshore waters, and the early colonists had to make money to pay off the backers who had financed their ocean voyage. Not many of them had been fishermen back home, but they learned how. They learned how to build ships, too, and by the time other colonies were established they were the merchant class. Their ships carried wheat from Pennsylvania and tobacco from Virginia

Vermont's Green Mountains celebrate fall.

to England, and they came back with their holds filled with the luxuries that made life in America a little more like home. The enterprising New England merchants also carried fish and lumber to the West Indies, where they traded it for sugar that they converted to rum in their own factories. The rum was in demand in Africa, where men were willing to trade it for other men, who were carried off to the Caribbean to be sold for gold as slaves to work the fields to produce more sugar to make more rum. It was like a perpetual motion machine, and the complex alchemy that turned sugar into gold created family fortunes that made Rhode Island and Massachusetts the richest colonies in the British Empire.

When the British began tightening the reins on the merchants with what they considered onerous taxes, revolution was inevitable, and it was just as inevitable that the flashpoint of the rebellion was the port of Boston. When the war was over, the New Englanders were free to trade anywhere they pleased, and it pleased them to range all over the world. For almost all of the 19th century American ships carried furs to China and spices from India to Europe. And almost all those ships made New England their home port. The sharp traders among them even created markets for things no one knew they needed, and blocks of New England ice packed in sawdust from New England trees became not only a convenient source of profit, but gave the world a taste for adding cubes of ice to their tea and their rum, both of which were carried to them in ships from New England.

The end of it all came in the 1880s, when steamships made even the great, fast clipper ships seem like slowpokes. Ironically, although the age of steam arrived on New York's Hudson River, the ships themselves evolved with the competition to build faster and more efficient steamers to carry passengers between New York and Boston past the Connecticut shore of Long Island Sound. Even the Mississippi River, whose steamboats became legendary, never saw the likes of the traffic that called at ports like Bridgeport and New London. No one knew at the time that the floating palaces spelled the decline of the New England ports, but even when they did, not much changed except the pace of life. It was still the most beautiful coastline in the country, and at the turn of the century Americans suddenly discovered that the seashore was a wonderful place to relax and enjoy life. Until then, relaxing and thinking of life as a joyful thing was vaguely sinful, and it was totally unpredictable that the idea would be discovered in New England.

But for lovers of the sea it is hard to imagine a better place. More than half the New England coast, 3,750 miles of inlets and coves in Maine, is rocky and dramatic, extending down past New Hampshire and into Massachusetts. The water is too cold even for wading and the tides are among the highest in the world. But everything changes at the point where Cape Cod stretches its arm fifty miles out into the sea. The Gulf Stream veers off to the east at that point, making the water as much as twenty degrees warmer south of the Cape. The landscape changes, too. Rocks are rare and the waves are held back by sand dunes and wide, inviting beaches. And the tides that rise and fall as much as ten feet in Cape Cod Bay vary less that two feet on Nantucket Sound.

The key word is variety. It is as much a part of the New England experience inland as on the coast. New England is the sum of many parts, six different states, three distinct geological regions and thirteen million people, some of whose ancestors arrived on the *Mayflower*, and others who came for a visit and decided to stay, but all of whom consider themselves individuals. They also consider themselves the luckiest of Americans, these New Englanders. At the heart of the experience is the basic philosophy summed up by James Russell Lowell when he said: "I stand by the old thought, the old thing, the old place and the old friend."

Ocean Beach at New London, Connecticut.

19

Hartford (above), Connecticut's capital, is home to more than 35 insurance companies as well as dozens of important industries, all adding to the excitement of its skyline. But for all its urban vitality, it is surrounded by such reminders of Connecticut's rural roots as this charming barn (right), defying both modern progress and the elements.

Connecticut's gold-domed capitol (left), and Hartford's City Hall (right) are both surrounded by the new landmarks of the city's ambitious urban redevelopment programs that have modernized Hartford, but left its historic traditions intact.

Mystic Seaport (above), on the Connecticut shore of Long
Island Sound, is the largest maritime museum in the country.
The nearby town of Mystic (right) was an important whaling
port and shipbuilding center for two centuries, and is still a
hard-working harbor.

In addition to its 19th-century whalers and fishing schooners, Mystic Seaport has an impressive collection of smaller vessels moored alongside an authentic New England seafaring community with historic homes and industries, including a working shipyard.

Long before it became famous as a posh summer resort,
Newport, Rhode Island, was a busy port. It still is.

Among the grand reminders of Newport's Gilded Age is Marble House (left), a Neo-Classical "cottage" designed by Richard Morris Hunt for William K. Vanderbilt in 1892. The Rhode Island State House (right) in Providence is another Classical masterpiece, designed by McKim, Mead and White nine years later.

The graceful Newport Bridge connects Newport with
Jamestown on the west side of Narragansett Bay. Its high
span has often provided a perfect backdrop for America's
Cup competitions.

The clock in the steeple of Newport's Trinity Church (above) has been counting the hours since 1726. But there never seem to be enough hours in any day to squeeze all the available pleasure out of cruising on the bay and following the gulls near Newport Bridge (right).

The harbor at Dartmouth (left), near New Bedford, Massachusetts, gives pleasure boaters access to the Atlantic through Rhode Island Sound as well as to Buzzard's Bay, where they might find a welcome at one of the houses on West Island (top right). At home, you might find them in a welcoming Cape Cod-style cottage behind a white picket fence.

Onset (left), at the head of Buzzard's Bay in Massachusetts, has fast boats in its marina, but the pace of life there is free, easy and relaxed. The same is true further west in Westport (right), near Fall River, where the sunsets can make life seem perfect.

The Pilgrim Monument at Provincetown, on the tip of Cape
Cod, not only marks the spot where the *Mayflower* first
anchored in 1620, but gives a wonderful view of the Cape
and, sometimes, of Plymouth across the bay.

41

Fishing vessels, both for professionals and visitors who find fishing a challenging sport rather than a way to make a living, crowd the harbor at Provincetown, where excursion boats also offer cruises, often in search of whales.

43

Nauset Beach (above) is part of the Cape Cod National
Seashore. The Cape's oldest town is Sandwich (right).

Cape Cod is 70 miles long, but it has 300 miles of shoreline, from the coves along Buzzard's Bay at West Falmouth (left), to the Ocean beaches and back around to Cape Cod Bay and towns like Dennis (right), where the wide-ranging tides can leave an anchored boat high and dry if its owner isn't careful.

Highland Light (above), near Truro, is on the site of Cape
Cod's first lighthouse. Its beacon can be seen from Nauset
Beach and from Pleasant Bay behind it (right).

Edgartown (left), the first settlement on the island of Martha's
Vineyard, was a rich whaling town in the 19th century.
Today, it is a resort popular with visitors who come to enjoy
such wonders as Gayhead Cliffs.

Chappaquiddick Island (left), at the southeast corner of Martha's Vineyard, is reached from Edgartown, near Katama Bay (right), on a ferry operating without a schedule, which is why her operator felt free to name her *On Time*. But time doesn't seem important on The Vineyard, one of the best places in New England to forget its pressures.

Great for vacations, Martha's Vineyard is also a great place to
live, and call a charming fishing village home.

ERECTED BY THE NATIONAL SOCIETY OF THE COLONIAL DAMES OF AMERICA TO
COMMEMORATE THE THREE HUNDREDTH ANNIVERSARY OF THE LANDING OF THE PILGRIMS

The Land of the Pilgrim's Pride is celebrated in Massachusetts by the marble-columned Classical temple sheltering Plymouth Rock, the stepping stone the Pilgrim fathers used when they first set foot in their new home. Modern Plymouth also includes Plimoth Plantation (bottom right), a reconstruction of the Commonwealth's first permanent settlement, and an operating replica of a 1636 grist mill (top right).

58

The First Church of Christ, Scientist (left), in Boston, is the world headquarters of the Christian Science movement, and of its Publishing Society, whose work includes the newspaper, *Christian Science Monitor*. And there isn't a better place to relax and catch up with the news than on a boat in the Charles River Basin under Longfellow Bridge (right).

The tower of Boston's Custom House rises above Long Wharf (left), where most of its revenues were once generated. The old sea captains who once trudged up the wharf to pay their duties probably wouldn't recognize Long Wharf today, but Quincy Market and Faneuil Hall (right) haven't changed much since 18th-century rebels gathered there to shake their fists in the direction of England.

The Cambridge campus of Harvard University (above), and
the Massachusetts Institute of Technology (right) – two
world-famous centers of higher education.

The Swan Boats in Boston's Public Garden (left) are as delightful a symbol of the city as the cobblestoned streets of Beacon Hill. In the winter months, they migrate indoors and the pond is filled with ice-skaters. The Weeks Memorial footbridge (right) over the Charles River connects Harvard's Cambridge campus with a river campus on the Boston side. Activity under it ranges from rowing and regattas to ice skating.

The Massachusetts coast is laced with safe harbors, from the one at Manchester (above left), on the top edge of Massachusetts Bay, to nearby Salem, whose Pickering Wharf (bottom left) is part of a National Historic Site, and the Port of Gloucester (right), whose fishing trawlers still take a huge harvest from the sea following a tradition dating back more than three centuries.

Vermont's capitol is of local granite, of course. Stowe (right)
is a symbol of another local industry: skiing.

Vermont has more than 7,000 farms and 251 small towns, many of which are so small you might miss them, but none so insignificant that you'll forget them. Almost a whole generation of visitors was lured there with a state promotion built on the theme, "Unspoiled Vermont," and although the slogan has changed, the Green Mountain State hasn't.

Vermont's Winooski River (above) has plenty of great
swimming holes, but come September, kids start looking for
ice and a whole new adventure. And soon the Green
Mountains will turn white and promise even more fun.

Based at the restored Victorian depot in the heart of North Conway, New Hampshire, the Conway Scenic Railroad offers a tour of the Saco River Valley that includes views of nearby Mount Washington. For a more lingering look at the 6,288-foot mountain P.T. Barnum called "The Second Greatest Show on Earth," visitors head for the Mount Washington Hotel (right).

New Hampshire's Washington Valley is always beautiful, but
never more so than on a crisp fall day.

New Hampshire's White Mountain National Forest has more than 1,125 miles of foot trails, many of which are within earshot of otherwise hidden creeks and streams and the Swift River (left). Glen Ellis Falls (right), near Pinkham Notch, is also in the National Forest, whose scenic wonders include eight mountain peaks more than a mile high.

Above: Conway, and (right) the state's capital, Concord.

One of New Hampshire's most beautiful mountain passes is Crawford Notch (right), a 15-mile valley created by the Saco River as it cuts through the White Mountains. Among the other rivers that work their soul-restoring wonders in the New Hampshire mountains is the aptly-named Swift River (left).

The Ellis River Valley (left) is part of the easternmost pass through New Hampshire's White Mountains. It has hardly changed since the early settlers used it as a west-bound highway. Equally unchanged is Echo Lake (above) and White Horse Ledge, near North Conway.

The village of Jackson, New Hampshire, at the southern end of Pinkham Notch, is a popular ski area, but folks who live in its tidy houses (left), or stay at the charming Whitneys' Village Inn (right), can't say when is the best time of year to enjoy it.

In 1790, Congress appropriated $1,500 to build Maine's Portland Head Light Station (left, and bottom right), and it has served almost unchanged ever since. The Cape Elizabeth Light (top right), built in 1828 as one of a pair marking the entrance to Casco Bay and Portland Harbor, lost its mate to an economy drive in the 1920s, in spite of a Lighthouse Board claim that the Cape Elizabeth station was the most important on the entire East Coast.

Boothbay Harbor, the heart of Maine's vacationland.

When the talk turns to quaint New England villages, Yarmouth (left), Maine, is sure to be included. And so is North Monmouth, set among the lakes due north of Portland. Like the rest of Maine, the two towns are completely unspoiled and relaxed, even though more than five million visitors go to the Pine Tree State each and every year.

Although much of Maine's 3,500 miles of coastline is rockbound, there are sandy beaches, too, including the seven miles of Old Orchard Beach (left), with its Palace Playland, an amusement park with a restored 1906 carousel, and a 475-foot pier filled with shops and restaurants. In other places, like Orrs Island (top right), the piers are shorter and more workmanlike and often, as in South Freeport (bottom right), boats pull up alongside neat bulkheads.

There may well be more boats than people in Maine, and they come in as many different sizes and shapes. For speed and comfort, a trim modern sea skiff (left) is just the ticket for pleasure on the water. But when there is work to be done, the lobstermen based at Port Clyde depend on their sturdier, but less racy, boats to make the rounds with their lobster pots.

Southwest Harbor (above) is one of a half-dozen villages on Maine's Mount Desert Island, whose seacapes include Bass Harbor Head Light, one of the most romantic lighthouses in America.

Cadillac Mountain, in Acadia National Park on Maine's Mount Desert Island is, at 1,530 feet, the highest point on the East Coast, and is often above the clouds, which makes it especially dramatic at sunrise (left). A few miles away, the same early light works magic with the boats anchored off Northeast Harbor (right). But as the sun rises past the yardarm, the boats along the shore (overleaf) seem eager to cut playful waves in the calm early morning water. And what a wonderful day it promises to be!